The
Charlie Chaplin
Walk

Dear Esther,

I hope that you enjoy the
story of this little boy
and see why I wanted to
tell his story.

With love & Best wishes

Stephen Smith
(a.k.a - Steve)

Published by Sigma Leisure – an imprint of
Sigma Press, Stobart House, Pontyclerc, Penybanc Road
Ammanford, Carmarthenshire SA18 3HP

British Library Cataloguing in Publication Data

A CIP record for this book is available from the British Library

ISBN: 978-1-85058-852-8

Typesetting and Design by: Sigma Press, Ammanford, Carms

Map: Bute Cartographics

Front Cover: Scenes from *The Tramp*

Printed by: Cromwell Press Group, Trowbrige, Wiltshire

Disclaimer: The information in this book is given in good faith and is believed to be correct at the time of publication. The author and publisher cannot take responsibility for any accidents or injury incurred whilst following these walks. Only you can judge your own fitness, competence and experience. Do not rely solely on sketch maps for navigation: we strongly recommend the use of appropriate London A to Z (or equivalent) maps.

The
Charlie Chaplin
Walk

Stephen P. Smith

Contents

Preface

As a boy of twelve, reading Charlie Chaplin's obituary in my parent's newspaper, I was surprised to learn that he was English. It was at a time when America was portrayed with such reverence that to claim him 'as our own' almost felt churlish. I felt embarrassed by the newsprint, as if somehow we'd be risking the wrath of our Atlantic neighbour. Then I felt proud that this boy, born and bred in London, should go on to be one of the greatest artists the cinema has ever produced.

In the early 1990s, the BBC showed a short season of Chaplin's work. I was transfixed by the genius of *Modern Times* and *City Lights* and, in a wish to discover more about the man, I read Chaplin's *My Autobiography*. I became fascinated by his early life and through my various readings, and an A to Z atlas, I tried to piece together the significant places of his childhood. This drew me more than anything else, but through all my enquiries, I could not find any book that would 'walk me around Lambeth', the place of his boyhood. So one Saturday, with many addresses scribbled in a notebook, I took the train into London and walked until my gait was akin to our comic hero. I felt a greater connection than through any book or documentary, to stand where he once stood, to look at the houses in which he once lived and to have the sense of déjà-vu that somehow this all looked rather familiar. For Chaplin's films are a portrayal of his childhood both in settings and experiences.

In this book we'll follow a walking tour, to be made on foot or in the comfort of an armchair, of many of the influential locations of his formative years. At the same time we will recall the childhood experiences that so shaped the man, actor and little Tramp. For the Tramp was cunning, astute at getting a minor advantage, and quick to walk away when the law was catching up. This is comedy tinged with tragedy creating great pathos with worldwide audiences. He was the master to make you laugh and cry all in one scene, the first to use the persistent retake to perfect, the first to slow the pace of the early films, both in production and speed of story, to feed into the Golden Age of Hollywood. Chaplin was a true genius, portraying the human element within us all. The films were silent and therefore had worldwide appeal – made by a man that came to regard himself as a citizen of the world.

There has been so much written about Chaplin that to produce a new work requires a different take on the events of his life. Firstly, as I've always held great interest in how one's childhood experiences shape the adult, I have focused on how his formative years influenced his films; other writings that mention the link tend to look at the films and work back to his childhood. Secondly this work enables fans to geographically travel around some of the places of his childhood, without flicking back and forth between biographies and *The A to Z*, to connect his childhood influences with his films.

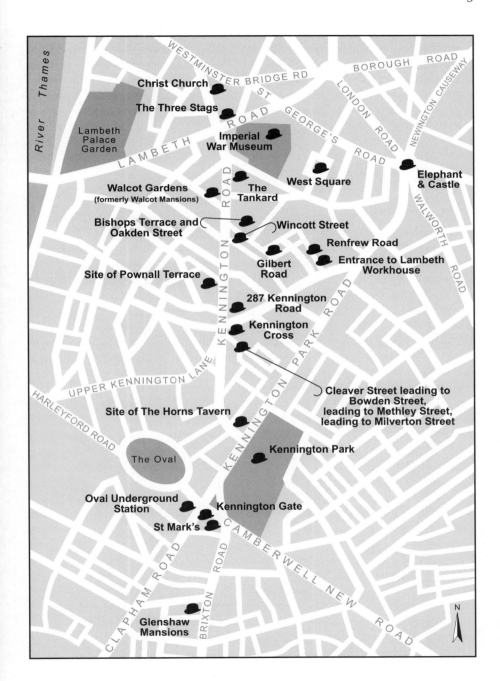

River Thames

WESTMINSTER BRIDGE RD

BOROUGH ROAD

NEWINGTON CAUSEWAY

ST GEORGE'S ROAD

LONDON ROAD

LAMBETH ROAD

Lambeth Palace Garden

Christ Church

The Three Stags

Imperial War Museum

West Square

Elephant & Castle

Walcot Gardens
(formerly Walcot Mansions)

The Tankard

WALWORTH ROAD

Bishops Terrace and Oakden Street

Wincott Street

Renfrew Road

Gilbert Road

Entrance to Lambeth Workhouse

Site of Pownall Terrace

KENNINGTON ROAD

287 Kennington Road

KENNINGTON PARK ROAD

Kennington Cross

UPPER KENNINGTON LANE

Cleaver Street leading to Bowden Street, leading to Methley Street, leading to Milverton Street

HARLEYFORD ROAD

Site of The Horns Tavern

KENNINGTON PARK ROAD

Kennington Park

The Oval

Oval Underground Station

Kennington Gate

St Mark's

CLAPHAM ROAD

BRIXTON ROAD

CAMBERWELL NEW ROAD

Glenshaw Mansions

N

1. Elephant and Castle

To begin the walk, take the Bakerloo Line on the London Underground to its most southerly destination, Elephant and Castle. Follow the exit signs for the Imperial War Museum, then the road underpass, and continue to follow the signs for the Imperial War Museum.

Michael Faraday Memorial on the old site of the Elephant and Castle pub – the birthplace of Chaplin's little Tramp

Once out of the underpass you are on St George's Road. If you turn and look into the centre of the road junction you'll see a stainless steel structure which is a memorial to another local man, the inventor Michael Faraday. This stands on the site of the Elephant and Castle pub, destroyed in a Second World War bombing raid.

In a 1918 article in *The Strand* magazine Charlie recalled:

> *I learned that big-foot shuffle and the ataxic walk from an old cab-horse tout in London, who used to hold horses outside the Elephant and Castle while the drivers were inside getting a*

drink. The old man was a physical wreck, but he had that comic walk and it used to amuse me, so I imitated it for the amusement of a few my friends. I'm glad I did. If it hadn't been for poor old Bill and his funny shuffle I should probably be knocking out twenty pounds a week or so as a vaudeville performer 'doing the provinces'.[1]

The Elephant and Castle pub as Charlie would have known it

2. West Square, St George's Road

West Square

Continue along St George's Road and take the first left after Hayles Street into West Square.

In Charlie's autobiography he says that soon after his birth the family moved to West Square:

Our circumstances were moderately comfortable; we lived in three tastefully furnished rooms.[2]

Standing in this square, built in 1791, one can see that this is an affluent area. Chaplin's autobiography begins:

I was born on April 16th 1889, at eight o'clock at night in East Lane, Walworth.[3]

We shall take East Lane to be the birthplace of Charles Spencer Chaplin although no Chaplin researcher has actually found the registration of his

Hannah Chaplin

birth. Charlie's father, Charles Chaplin and his mother, the actress Lily Harvey, who was born Hannah Harriet Hill, were both music hall performers. They married in June 1885, their address being given as the now demolished 57 Brandon Street (probably bombed during the Second World War). Charlie's half brother, Sydney, had been born four years previously to a different father but was given the family name of Chaplin upon the marriage. Sydney and Charlie were to become very close brothers who stood by one another through the tragedy and poverty of their childhoods.

We'll discover on our walking tour that some areas remain just as Charlie would have remembered, whereas, due to the bomb damage of the Second World War, others have changed beyond recognition. East Lane (now East Street) is such a victim, with the likely place of Chaplin's birth now gone. There is just a poorly placed plaque, on the junction of Walworth Road and East Street. East Lane, until the mid nineteenth century, was at the other end of East Street between Flint Street and the Old Kent Road[4]. As it was not unusual for Londoners to still use the original name of a renamed street – probably out of a lack of respect for an authority that did little for them – it's not surprising that Charlie regarded himself as having been born in East Lane. A lane frequently depicted the place of a market and East Street still has a market but it's now on the Walworth Road end.

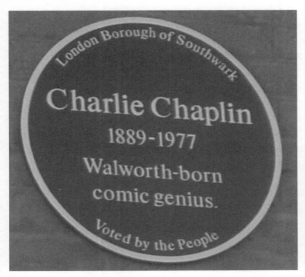

The plaque on the corner of Walworth Road and East Street (the place of Charlie's birth). Although Charlie was born in the borough of Walworth he grew up in the neighbouring borough of Lambeth

Charlie Chaplin lived in and around this area until he set sail for America in 1910 to tour with the Fred Karno troupe. He grew up in difficult circumstances, yet through the poverty and tragedy of his childhood, and early music hall training, he created his famous Tramp character, the world icon of silent cinema. Pictorially the Tramp was a combination of the men he had seen in the streets and music halls of London, but his character was born of his experiences.

America was to be where Charlie found his fame and fortune but as we will see, what made Charlie famous was the portrayal of the poverty from the streets of his youth.

Many of his films show him getting a free meal, a free drink or one up on authority in comical ways. Charlie's sympathies often lie with the poor and downtrodden of society. He learned choreography from his parents, and his sentimental portrayals were drawn from the tragedies around him. His early films often could be described as stage shows from the music hall. However, Chaplin took silent movies further than anybody else had ever done. The Tramp was anarchic, anti-authority and took any opportunity to kick somebody 'up the rear'.

We'll now turn our attention to West Square. There have been some unproven references that Chaplin lived here in number 39. Many actors of the music hall era would have lived in these districts, south of the river. It was a time before radio, television and even the cinema, so live entertainment was in high demand. When things were going well one would aspire to live in a place such as this. Just a quarter of a mile south was Lambeth Workhouse, the place for the destitute of the parish. The distance between wealth and poverty was never more than a few streets.

1890 was a time when Charlie's father was successful and drinking; even entertaining in America, where years later Charlie was to make his name. Alcohol and the music halls were synonymous, with the actors being paid excessive salaries to enable them to drink with the patrons after the performance. It was common for music halls, whose roots lay in entertainment room additions to public houses, to make more profit from the drink sales than the admission price. Unfortunately Charles Chaplin Senior slipped into alcoholism.

In August 1892 George Dryden Wheeler, later known as Wheeler Dryden, was born to Hannah; taking the name of his music hall father, Leo Dryden.[5] The marriage to Charlie's father had, by this time, failed; it's unclear whether the liaison with Leo Dryden caused the break up or whether Chaplin Senior's alcoholism had already caused the demise of the relationship. The 1891 census shows Charlie living with his mother and grandmother in Barlow Street at an address now gone (another likely victim of the Second World War), and the father living elsewhere.[6] These were not yet hard times as their mother would tuck the boys in before going off to perform at music halls, leaving them in the care of a housemaid.

Wheeler was snatched by his father, Leo Dryden, in the spring of 1893 and taken to live in Africa.[7] Hannah surely suffered badly over this but protected Sydney and Charlie who recalled nothing of the pregnancy or birth. Hannah was to have no further contact with her son for around thirty years until Wheeler, realising he was Charlie's brother made persistent contact. Wheeler, like Sydney, had his own modest film career and eventually worked with Charlie in some of his later films.

Hannah was adept at protecting the boys, even when her own mother fell ill around this time and ended up in the workhouse and then the lunatic asylum. Up until the mid 1890s, and despite a larynx condition, Hannah continued to work as a music hall singer with Charlie sometimes going along and watching from the wings. Charlie's first stage appearance was an impromptu performance at the age of five or six. Hannah was performing at *The Canteen* theatre in Aldershot, frequented by unforgiving soldiers, when her voice gave way. She was booed, jeered and pelted off stage. Upset and angry, she argued with the stage manager. The stage manager, knowing that Charlie could sing, led the five-year-old Chaplin on to the stage and he started singing a popular tune at that time, *Jack Jones*. The little boy did so well, even faking a cracking voice to imitate his mother that the audience showered him with coins which he broke his performance to gather. Charlie recalls:

> *That night was my first appearance on the stage and Mother's last.*[8]

The money raised was far from enough to maintain the family for Charlie recalls:

*Meanwhile from three comfortable rooms we moved into two,
then into one, our belongings dwindling and the
neighbourhoods into which we moved growing progressively
drabber.*[9]

We can look to some of Charlie's films to get a sense of his life at the time. Although the 1918 film *Shoulder Arms* is about the First World War, it reveals despair through comedy. There is a trench scene showing multiple occupancy beds; likely a feature of Charlie's boyhood. Depravity and comedy are close by and Chaplin had the genius to reveal it in his work.

In the 1925 film, *The Gold Rush*, perhaps the film for which he is most remembered, he depicts not eating for days on end and has the audience roaring with laughter when he boils and eats his boot. In his autobiography he tells how his mother sold an oil stove to a passing rag and bone man so they could eat. The theme of poverty and hunger reoccurs across his films. For Chaplin, unlike the London of today, the two were synonymous.

3. Christ Church

Return to St George's Road and turn left. Cross Lambeth Road, at the crossing lights and keep on St George's road for a short distance, then turn left into Westminster Bridge Road. On the junction of Westminster Bridge Road and Kennington Road is Christ Church, which Hannah attended with Charlie (she became more religious after the loss of her voice and theatrical friends). Charlie recalls the boring sermons, though Hannah sought sustenance from religion and the small amount of money she earned through dressmaking and nursing for other congregation members.

This was a time with no welfare state, and a woman without the support of a man could be thrust into poverty. Chaplin's father's support was infrequent and begrudgingly given. Though unable to perform herself, Hannah entertained Charlie and Sydney with her old music hall songs. Undoubtedly this was Charlie's early training and he readily acknowledged that much of his talent was from his petite, refined mother's ability to perform. The Tramp became the conduit of all that he had learned both on and off the streets.

Christ Church was built between 1873 and 1876 but was badly bomb damaged during the Second World War, hence the later addition attached to the surviving tower. If you stand and look around you can begin to see how badly this area was hit in the blitz. Opposite on the junction with Hercules Road you can still see the gap in the buildings where a bomb fell. Hitler may have shaped London more than Charlie but London certainly shaped Charlie.

Born just four days apart, Chaplin and Adolf Hitler both had major impacts on the twentieth century. Hitler may have copied the mass appeal of Charlie's moustache but it was Charlie who stole the victory in the 1940 film, The *Great Dictator*, where he parodied Adolf Hitler as Adenoid Hynkel and the sign of the double cross. Here is a common theme of Chaplin's work: the ridicule of power and authority. Through the use of comedy Chaplin could bring to the screen the horror of what was happening in central Europe. Where politicians and Hollywood faltered, Chaplin had the courage to show Hitler in an unflattering light. In the film

Christ Church

Chaplin plays two parts, Hynkel and a Jewish barber who are very similar in looks. What a dig at Hitler that he could be mistaken for a Jewish barber. Inevitably the two are mistaken and the barber is able to make a radio speech, in the place of Hynkel, crying out for hope. Though a plea about the brutality of fascism, it does touch on the sentiment of Chaplin's youth as the lady the Jewish barber falls for in the film (Paulette Goddard, Chaplin's then wife), is called Hannah and the film portrays the downtrodden as bullied by authority. In his famous speech across the airwaves, he says, 'Hannah, can you hear me? Wherever you are, look up Hannah. The clouds are lifting, the sun is breaking through.' It's unlikely to be coincidence that Chaplin's leading ladies and wives bore a resemblance to his dark-haired mother Hannah. In *Limelight* Charlie's then wife, Oona O'Neill, briefly substituted for his leading lady, the actress Claire Bloom.

Around the time of the release of *The Great Dictator*, there was pressure on Charlie to reveal whether he was Jewish. Concerned that a denial from a global star would further alienate the Jewish people, he reportedly replied with, 'I do not have that honour.' A half-Roma grandmother was the likely reason Charlie's looks were often mistaken as Jewish.

4. The Three Stags

Take the road that passes the church to its right and start to stroll down what is Kennington Road, the most significant area of Charlie's childhood. Keep to the left and, at the junction with Lambeth Road you'll find The Three Stags pub. As we are passing we'll jump ahead five or six years to 1901 and quote from his autobiography:

The Three Stags in Kennington Road was not a place my father frequented, yet as I passed it one evening an urge prompted me to peek inside to see if he was there. I opened the saloon door just a few inches, and there he was, sitting in the corner! I was about to leave, but his face lit up and he beckoned me to him. I was surprised at such a welcome, for he was never demonstrative. He looked ill; his eyes were sunken, and his body

The Three Stags – inside is a Chaplin's Corner

Charlie Chaplin Senior

*had swollen to an enormous size. He rested one hand,
Napoleon-like, in his waistcoat as if to ease his difficult
breathing. That evening he was most solicitous, enquiring after
Mother and Sydney, and before I left took me in his arms and
for the first time kissed me. That was the last time I saw him
alive.*[10]

A matter of weeks later, on May 9th 1901, aged thirty seven, Charles
Senior died in St Thomas's Hospital, from liver cirrhosis and dropsy.
Charlie's mother visited him towards the end and, upon his death, was
asked who would bury him. She was unable to afford a funeral and his
family would not have the humiliation of a charity burial so his brother,
an Uncle Albert visiting from Africa, covered the costs.

On the day of the funeral they collected the body from St Thomas's
hospital, Hannah arriving early as she wanted to see her husband before
they closed the lid. She attended the funeral, at Tooting cemetery, with
just Charlie – Sydney was working and Charles Senior was not his
biological father. The Chaplin family were icy towards them, asking where
they wanted to be dropped before going for their own pub lunch.

For a few weeks after the funeral Charlie would buy flowers and make
them into penny bundles and sell them around the pubs. With a mourning
armband, he played the role well and made a good profit. This was until
Hannah caught him, scolded him for visiting the pubs that killed his
father, forbade him to sell flowers again and kept the proceeds.

As you cross the road, keeping on Kennington Road, note the signpost
for Chaplin Mews. To the left you will see the Imperial War Museum.

5. The Tankard, Kennington Road

The Tankard

Continue a short way down Kennington Road, passing the open area to your left. The road on your left is Brook Drive and in the triangle formed with it and Kennington Road is The Tankard. Look high up to see its sign. In Chaplin's autobiography he gives us an interesting insight into this area:

> *Before Westminster Bridge was open, Kennington Road was only a bridle path. After 1750, a new road was laid down from the Bridge forming a direct link to Brighton. As a consequence Kennington Road, where I spent most of my boyhood, boasted some fine houses of architectural merit, fronted with iron grill balconies from which occupants could once have seen George IV coaching on his way to Brighton.*[11]

To this day Kennington Road remains as the A23 connecting road between London and Brighton. Charlie goes on to say:

> *By the middle of the nineteenth century most of the homes had deteriorated into rooming houses and apartments. Some, however, remained inviolate and were occupied by doctors, successful merchants and vaudeville stars. On Sunday morning, along the Kennington Road one could see a smart pony and trap outside a house, ready to take a vaudevillian for a ten-mile drive as far as Norwood or Merton, stopping on the way back at the various pubs, the White Horse, the Horns and the Tankard in the Kennington Road.*

> *As a boy of twelve, I often stood outside the Tankard watching these illustrious gentlemen alight from their equestrian outfits to enter the lounge bar, where the elite of the vaudeville met, as was their custom on a Sunday to take a final 'one' before going home to the midday meal. How glamorous they were, dressed in chequered suits and grey bowlers, flashing their diamond rings and tie-pins! At two o'clock Sunday afternoon, the pub closed and its occupants filed outside and dallied awhile before bidding each other adieu; and I would gaze fascinated and amused, for some of them swaggered with a ridiculous air.*

> *When the last had gone his way, it was as though the sun had gone under a cloud. And I would return to a row of old derelict houses sat back off Kennington Road, to 3 Pownall Terrace, and mount the rickety stairs that led to our small garret.*

We'll visit the site of 3 Pownall Terrace later. We can deduce, from the area's mix of lower standard multiple occupancy dwellings and some still occupied by the well-to-do, that Charlie was always on the fringes of poverty and wealth, as so often was the Tramp.

In his films Charlie told the story through a fixed camera position, perhaps influenced by the observations of the static wide-eyed little boy peering out from the shadows of the slums; close-ups and clever camera angles were not his style.

Houses on opposite side of road between Brook Drive and Wincott Street

After our diversion past these public houses we'll now return to the chronology of our story, the mid-1890s. Charlie remembers living in a one-room basement. Although he remembers this as Oakley Street[12] it is likely to be Oakden Street, which is just off Bishop's Terrace next to The Ship further down Kennington Road. He was recovering from fever and his mother read to him from the Bible, bringing the text to life as she imagined the different characters' voices. Her reading was so good, making a better narrator than the minister of Christ Church; she ended up having to persuade Charlie that he should not wish upon himself a premature death so he could be with Jesus. In his 1923 film, *The Pilgrim*, Charlie performs, before a church congregation, an exaggerated recital of David and Goliath and one wonders if this is Hannah's influence.

As they sunk further into poverty Hannah kept the family's pride afloat by correcting the boys' diction and grammar. She may have only been able to provide her boys with accommodation befitting her poor purse, but

Scene From Chaplin's *Limelight* complete with barrel organ; a familiar part of Victorian London street life

she was determined to provide her boys with an education that rose above that of the neighbourhood.

Hannah continued to do needlework for a pittance and Charlie would see her at her happiest when she talked about her life on the stage. This, and his Sunday observations of vaudeville stars outside The Tankard, was Charlie's cue that the stage brought good things in an otherwise impoverished life.

Walk further down Kennington Road, pausing to look at some of the fine houses opposite that Charlie referred to in his autobiography.

6. Lambeth Workhouse

Take the third left, after Brook Drive, into Wincott Street, left into Gilbert Road then follow the road round to the right into what becomes Renfrew Road. Note the modern buildings on your left occupying part of the old site of Lambeth Workhouse. On your left, opposite the Cotton Garden Estate, is the short and unmarked Dugard Way. This is the main entrance to the former Lambeth Workhouse where two small gatehouses mark the entrance.

Lambeth Workhouse

Hannah's fortunes spiralled downwards. Charlie's father ceased his payment of ten shillings a week. She started having migraines and when she became unable to work, her sewing machine was repossessed. She sought legal guidance and was advised to seek support from the Lambeth Borough authorities: this meant the workhouse. The family were to spend

Workhouse water tower

time both here in the Lambeth Workhouse and the Newington Workhouse on Westmoreland Road. A workhouse was for people unable to sustain themselves. They were designed to be as unattractive as possible with dormitory accommodation, separation of men, women and children and a rough workhouse uniform. Food was basic, such as gruel, bread and cheese. The able-bodied had to work at breaking stones or picking apart old ropes. Charlie recalls:

> *Although we were aware of the shame of going to the workhouse, when Mother told us about it both Sydney and I thought it adventurous and a change from living in one stuffy room. But on the doleful day I didn't realise what was happening until we actually entered the workhouse gate. Then the forlorn bewilderment of it struck me for there we were made to separate, Mother going in one direction to the women's ward and we in another to the children's.*[13]

Look up at the austerity of the old water tower, the brick tower with the dark capping. Standing out as it does, an ironic beacon to the poor, it would not have looked out of place on the drawing board of Albert Speer. Charlie goes on to say:

> *How well I remember the poignant sadness of that first visiting day: the shock of seeing Mother enter the visiting-room garbed in workhouse clothes. How forlorn and embarrassed she looked! In one week she had aged and grown thin, but her face lit up when she saw us. Sydney and I began to weep which made Mother weep, and large tears began to run down her cheeks.*

In his 1921 film, *The Kid*, Charlie shows a mother who is not able to support her child, poignantly referred to in an intertitle as, 'The woman whose sin was motherhood.' In this film the friendless and outcast Tramp 'adopts' an unwanted child, whom he raises as his own – two lonely humans finding love from each other. The authorities come to take the child away to a loveless institution causing the boy to become distressed. The Tramp, the surrogate father, is half crazed with grief and this is possibly one of the most tear-jerking scenes in film history. This is Chaplin's genius; creating audience pathos and using comedy and tragedy side by side.

The parallel between this scene in *The Kid* and Charlie's entrance into the workhouse is obvious but there is also the analogous snatching of Wheeler from his mother; for by the time Charlie made *The Kid* he had become aware of Wheeler's existence and was likely aware of the circumstances in which the boy was taken from his mother.

**The distress of *The Kid* as the authorities are about to take him away,
in the back of a truck, to a loveless institution**

London was a cruel place in those days. The workhouse brought shame, the sick and derelict were mocked in the streets. Even to be seen in poor clothes was a source of embarrassment. Though in Charlie's autobiography we can see touching moments of kindness offered to this poor young boy. In his 1947 film, *Monsieur Verdoux*, the world is described as 'a blundering world and a very sad one yet a little kindness can make it beautiful.'

Monsieur Verdoux is a dark film based on the French serial killer, Landru. In his autobiography Charlie recounts, as a boy, perceptively declining

GENTLEMAN TRAMP © Roy Export Company Establishment 1975

An 1896 photo of Charlie taken whilst at Hanwell School. He attended Hanwell from 1896 to 1898

a glass of water from one George Chapman who, two weeks later, was charged with murdering five wives. George Chapman is thought to be a strong candidate for Jack the Ripper as out of all the possible suspects he was proven to be a serial killer of women. One of the Ripper's early victims, Mary Ann Nichols, was actually once an inmate here at Lambeth Workhouse and it was possible that Charlie would have heard these tales that later became an influence on *Monsieur Verdoux*. The Verdoux character has an invalid wife, who he loves, who talks of the fear of poverty and returning to one room. He marries and murders rich women to support her. This is an interesting connection with the younger Chaplin and his mother, as the woman Verdoux truly loves is an invalid who fears returning to the poverty of living in one room. Chaplin plays the part of a man prepared to kill to prevent that from happening.

While under the care of the authorities the boys were to spend time both at the distant Norwood School and the Central London District School at Hanwell for Orphans and Destitute Children. At Hanwell (a Poor Law institution built in 1856 to receive children from inner city London) the feelings of adventure soon wore thin as Sydney, being older, was separated from Charlie. Though he worked in the kitchen and would slip Charlie extra food whenever he could, this unfortunately did not last long as Sydney was transferred to the training ship, Exmouth.

Although Hanwell was a nicer area, Charlie inevitably felt very sad at the separation from his mother and brother. The boys were taken for walks in the country lanes, hundreds of them, at two abreast, with the locals staring. Now aged seven, he witnessed cruel public floggings for punishments. Boys were advised to admit to a charge even if innocent as to plead not guilty would inevitably bring more lashes. Charlie was falsely accused of setting fire to the lavatory; he pleaded guilty and received three excruciating strokes to his behind. In his films the Tramp was often accused of things he was not guilty of.

Kicking oppressors and bullies up the rear, snubs at authority became the mainstay of many of Charlie's films. They would always get a laugh as the poor masses, to which he appealed, would applaud his revenge. The Tramp was often portrayed as winning through even if his oppressors did not spot his victory. Survival in institutional life was about minor victories.

In the 1923 film, *A Woman of Paris*, there's an intertitle which says:

> *Note: – Truffles rooted up from the soil by hogs – A delicacy for pigs and gentlemen.*

This is a typical Chaplin dig with clever use of the word gentlemen and not just men. Indeed he was quite cheeky. *A Woman of Paris* depicts wealth but is never far from Chaplin's roots. As the mistress of a wealthy playboy ponders motherhood, by way of an intertitle 'I want a real home, babies, and a man's respect', a window is opened and she is encouraged to observe an impoverished family, with a disengaged father and a mother trying to keep the children together, crossing the street below.

Hanwell School, now a community centre, is to this day a depressing and austere Victorian creation. Now on Cuckoo Avenue it was known as a "Cuckoo School" because children were left in the care of others. It is near to Castle Bar Park railway station which can be reached from London Paddington

At Hanwell the boys received just an orange for Christmas and apparently Charlie never really celebrated Christmas; he died on Christmas day 1977. This poor diet was a probable contributor to Charlie contracting ringworm, which required his head to be shaved, a dousing of iodine and isolation from the healthy boys. Those infected would be loathed and taunted by the healthy inmates. The isolation of the downtrodden is regularly highlighted in his films. In *The Gold Rush* and *City Lights* the Tramp is bullied and taunted because of his status. One quote from his autobiography makes interesting reading:

> *Mother stopped to upbraid some boys tormenting a derelict woman who was grotesquely ragged and dirty. She had a cropped head, unusual in those days, and the boys were*

laughing and pushing each other towards her, as if to touch her would contaminate them. The pathetic woman stood like a stag at bay until Mother interfered. Then a look of recognition came over the woman's face. 'Lil,' she said, feebly referring to Mother's stage name, 'don't you know me – Eva Lestock.'

Mother recognised her at once, an old friend of her vaudeville days.

I was so embarrassed that I moved on and waited for Mother at the corner. The boys walked past me, smirking and giggling.[14]

What is depicted here is the shame and embarrassment of falling on hard times and the reinforcement that failure as an artist meant absolute poverty.

Charlie's mother, having managed to leave the workhouse, visited during this isolation. She then got the three of them into a room at Kennington Park.

7. 287 Kennington Road

Continue to the end of Renfrew Road and turn right into Kennington Lane. Proceed to the junction with Kennington Road, turn right by The Dog House pub, and stop at number 287, with the grey plaque. In the late 1890s this was a boarding house where Charles Chaplin Senior, his mistress Louise and their small son stayed on the first floor. Note the incorrect year of Chaplin's death on the plaque. Although well presented today, some home cinema, shot by Charlie's wife Oona in the 1950s, shows it in the rundown state more akin to Charlie's boyhood. The rundown nature of the streets, with the Tramp walking amongst rubbish and the decay of the neighbourhood, are well depicted in *The Kid*. Only in recent years has the area taken on the gentrified look it has now.

Hannah failed to find employment and come 1898 they were moving from one backroom hovel to another, fighting to survive. Charles Senior was continually chased, by the district relief committee, for not maintaining his family and was even arrested for this, yet often managed to evade payments. By 1898 the authorities were doubling their efforts in chasing him. In September 1898, with Hannah in poor mental health in Cane Hill Asylum, the boys were released into the care of Charlie's father, here at 287 Kennington Road.[15] Charlie recalls:

> *The prospect of living with Father was exciting. I had seen him only twice in my life, on stage, and once when passing a house in Kennington Road, as he was coming down the front garden path with a lady. I had paused and watched him, knowing instinctively he was my father. He beckoned me to him and asked my name. Sensing the drama of the situation, I had feigned innocence and said: 'Charlie Chaplin'. Then he glanced knowingly at the lady, felt in his pocket and gave me half a crown, and without further ado I ran straight home and told Mother that I had met my father.*[16]

When the boys arrived here Charlie's father's sullen mistress, Louise, and four-year-old son, greeted them. It was to be a brief stay with little contact with the boy. Louise was a heavy drinker and made Sydney's life difficult though she was reasonable with Charlie. One wonders if this is because

287 Kennington Road

her son and Charlie were half-brothers, whereas this was not the case with Sydney. The only positive for Charlie was watching his father doing his vaudeville impressions (though his habit of swallowing six raw eggs, soaked in port wine, at a time probably did less to endear himself to his son).

Charlie recalls drunken rows between his father and the gloomy Louise. He must have missed his own joyful mother, so when one day Hannah called for her boys, they grabbed their things when the landlady went to fetch them. Louise and Hannah were too embarrassed to meet, though both were equally happy with the new arrangement.

8. Methley Street

Backtrack down Kennington Road, crossing the Kennington Lane, and take the first left into Cleaver Street, on the corner with The White Hart pub followed by an immediate right into Bowden Street. To your right is the former factory building, City Lights Court, named after Charlie's 1931 film, *City Lights*. Straight ahead of you, boasting a blue plaque is 39 Methley Street. As you can see, Charlie lived here from 1898 to 1899 and this was the place where Hannah took her two boys after collecting them from Charlie's father at 287 Kennington Road.

39 Methley Street

Although this now looks like a well-to-do area, in Victorian London it was a drab abode, next to a slaughterhouse and pickle factory whose buildings still remain in Bowden Street. Abattoirs were not sanitised places miles out of town, with meat being brought in by refrigerated lorry, but instead everything was handled locally so that the meat could be consumed soon after slaughter. The houses were not owner-occupied by financiers and media consultants, but rented by working class people, employed in local businesses. Therefore imagination is required to picture this setting as Charlie would have known it.

Despite the poorer surroundings, all parties were happy, and Chaplin Senior's ten shillings a week contribution came through. Perhaps, realising the consequences of the boys living with him again, the contribution was a price worth paying for domestic peace with Louise.

Hannah took up her sewing again and renewed her contact with the church. Sydney found employment as a telegraph boy, which, as Charlie recalled, gave his brother a uniform to wear during the week. Every Monday, in a bid to make ends meet, Hannah would place Sydney's weekend suit in the pawnshop until it became so threadbare the broker would no longer lend on it. Chaplin later celebrated this feature of London life in his 1916 film, *The Pawn Shop* and also made reference to the pawnbroker in the Tramp's gibberish song at the end of his 1936 film *Modern Times* (this is the only time the Tramp spoke).

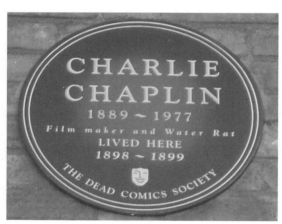

Methley Street plaque

Their Methley Street landlady, a Mrs J Crane, later recalled:

> *Mrs Chaplin and her boys stayed at numerous addresses round and about the Horns Hotel, Kennington, Chester Street, Oakden*

Street, Pownall Terrace and Methley Street, many of them now gone in the blitz, were the kind of places they lived in for a few weeks when they had some money.

The family had a one attic room with me. When she couldn't get singing engagements, poor Mrs. Chaplin worked all day at needlework, making blouses for a few pennies each. She had a hard job making ends meet.

The older boy, Sydney worked for the Post Office, I think. Charles was rather a frail child with his mop of dark hair, his pale face and bright blue eyes. He was what I call a 'little limb' – out in the streets from morning to night.

I remember he was a regular one for finding a man with a barrel organ and dancing to the music. He got a lot of extra money for the organ grinder and a few coppers for himself. I suppose that's how he started becoming an entertainer. Charlie was supposed to go to school in Kennington, but he was an awful truant.[17]

What an insight this article is. These few words portray the early life of Chaplin more than any words written over a hundred years later. Although Mrs Crane recalls Charlie being an 'awful truant' it was at school, whilst living here at Methley Street, he made his first true debut in reciting 'Miss Priscilla's Cat'. His mother had seen it outside a newspaper shop and had copied it down. A teacher overheard Charlie reciting it to others and within a day he was reciting it to every class in the school. What's also interesting is the revelation that Charlie was out in the streets from morning to night. In *The Kid* we see a familiar pattern of the Tramp wandering the streets, with the intertitle 'His Morning Promenade', escaping the despair of his one- room hovel.

In Charlie's autobiography he recalls:

An incident stands out at that period. At the end of our street was a slaughter-house, and sheep would pass our house on their way to be butchered. I remember one escaped and ran down the street to the amusement of onlookers. Some tried to grab it and others tripped over themselves. I had giggled with delight at its lambent capering and panic, it seemed so comic. But when it was caught and carried back into the slaughter-house, the reality of the tragedy came over me and I ran indoors, screaming and weeping to Mother: 'They're going to kill it! They're going to kill it!' That stark, spring afternoon and that comedy chase stayed with me for days; and I wonder if that episode did not establish the premise of my future films – the combination of the tragic and the comic.[18]

This indeed was very likely an influence on Charlie's films as the chase scene was common to early cinema and Chaplin certainly had this experience to draw upon. In the 1928 film, *The Circus* we see the comedy chase taken a stage further with it becoming an accidental act within a circus performance.

Standing here one can see the inspiration for the street scenes in *The Kid*. In it the Tramp adopts a baby he finds abandoned in the streets and the impoverished, yet ever resourceful Hannah shines through when the Tramp improvises a watering can with a teat and a chair with a hole with a pot underneath.

In his films Chaplin was as much an improviser as he was in early life trying to make money around the streets of Lambeth. Not only as an actor and director (a frequent music hall combination) but the Tramp himself would often turn an everyday object into something else. This resourcefulness can only come from deprivation and poverty where to survive one had to extract the most from every object and in every child of poverty is the dream of great riches. While the Tramp continued to play the role of the downtrodden, down-on-his-luck hero, the studios that Chaplin built were a London boy's dream of rich London suburban facades. Chaplin said:

I became rich by imitating the most poorest of men.

The Kid mixes slapstick and sentiment brilliantly. It's the work of a true storyteller that can have you laughing one moment and crying the next. As already mentioned, *The Kid* so movingly engenders the separation of a child from a parent, such as Charlie and Hannah experienced at the workhouse gates. The child in the film yearned for a father, as Chaplin would probably have yearned for his. Using nearly every single emotion

Scene from *The Kid* showing a façade common to the side streets off Kennington Road

possible *The Kid* made cinematic history, by its length and how it told the story. Instead of being the typical 'short' (one or two reels of film), it was a full six-reel film and took over a year to make. This compares with some of Chaplin's early films that were shot in less than a day.

In *The Kid*, the estranged father of the child lights a pipe with a burning photograph of the mother and we can only wonder if this flippancy was a recollection of the attitude of Charlie's own father. A further parallel with *The Kid* and Charlie's relationship with his brother Sydney, is the scene where two of the minor characters portray brothers, with the older always sticking up for the smaller younger one.

Jackie Coogan, the child star of *The Kid*, was the son of vaudeville stars and had come on at the end of one of his father's performances. Chaplin witnessed this and could not wait to sign him up for the movies. In many ways Chaplin would have seen Coogan as his younger self, the professions

Scene from *The Kid*. The little boy in the photo, who played the kid, is Jackie Coogan and is a major star of the film. Fans of the 1960s TV series *The Addams Family* might be surprised to learn that Jackie Coogan played the part of Uncle Fester

of both parents and the setting he put him in *The Kid*. Chaplin's method of working was to act out the scene for the actor, even down to every facial movement. With certain players this would lead to great conflict but Jackie Coogan could repeat it back perfectly.

If we look again at Jackie Coogan's entrance onto the stage we can now look at another parallel with the early life of Chaplin. In late 1898, Charlie's father asked William Jackson who led a clog-dancing troupe, known as "The Eight Lancashire Lads", if he would employ Charlie. Hannah took a bit of convincing to allow Charlie to join but Charles Senior argued that their son would get board and lodging, the start of a career and Hannah would get half a crown a week. He probably failed to mention that this would likely mean he could escape making his own payments.

The Eight Lancashire Lads worked two or three London music halls a night and would also spend time touring, so the boys would change school each week. Clog dancing, requiring perfect synchronisation, was popular in the industrial north, entertaining and funny to watch. Charlie was a natural. Perhaps this perfectionism was what caused Chaplin to

Charlie while touring with The Eight Lancashire Lads

do the constant retake in his films. He also used the retake to perfect a story, starting with no script and building a story take by take. It's possible that this reflected his unscripted life as a child where planning ahead was impossible and survival required just making the smartest move in the circumstances.

Scene from *Easy Street*

The view down Milverton Street

The 1901 census places Charlie as living away from his mother. In his autobiography Charlie says:

> *When we were in London, I visited Mother every week-end. She thought I looked pale and thin and that dancing was affecting my lungs. It worried her so much that she wrote about it to Mr Jackson, who was so indignant that he finally sent me home, saying that I was not worth the bother of such a worrying mother.*[19]

Sydney was at sea, using the qualifications he'd picked up on the training ship. This was a cause of sadness for Charlie as his brother was away for long periods of time. It did mean that money was fleetingly more secure, though they soon became impoverished again and Charlie, developing asthma, was often bedridden. Shortly before his father's death, Hannah and Charlie ended up in attic rooms at the rather downmarket 3 Pownall

Scene from *A Dog's Life* showing the classic T-shaped road formation common to Lambeth

The view down Exon Street

Terrace, with Sydney joining them when he was home on leave. Hannah's values to keep her family together, and Sydney's clear wish to be part of that, clearly influenced the young Chaplin. His connection with Sydney was lifelong, he later accepted Wheeler as his brother and he brought Hannah to America for the latter years of her life. As a tribute to his family Charlie named his first two surviving sons Charles and Sydney.

To find the site of Pownall Terrace we'll first turn right into Milverton Street. As you get to Gateway House, the modern building on your left, stop, turn around and look back up Milverton Street. Compare what you see with the still from Charlie's 1917 film, *Easy Street*, and 1918 film *A Dog's Life*. Similar scenes can be found around the area but this is right next to where Charlie lived and played. There's a similar setting, where two roads form a T, when looking down Exon Street from East Street, where Charlie was born. Although Charlie was very small when he left East Street his grandparents were still recorded as living there when he was old enough to remember.[20]

Whether the film's name, *Easy Street*, was a coincidence or a conscious choice from the place of his birth the scenes are definitely of London streets. In the story the police would not dare patrol the area and it takes one of their own, Chaplin, to clean it up.

9. Pownall Terrace

Follow the road around to the right, towards the traffic lights, back into Kennington Road, then cross Kennington Lane, keeping on the right side of the road passing The Dog House pub and number 287 again. When you reach number 235, next to Chester House, stop and look across the road. Opposite stands a petrol station, immediately to the left there is a small tree on the pavement. The tree stands approximately on the site of the doorway of 3 Pownall Terrace. The buildings that stood here have now gone but this site is still worth a visit as it was a significant place for Charlie.

The family had a tiny top floor room in what was a three-story house, virtually opposite where the boys previously stayed with Charlie's father.

Scene from the Tramp's attic room in *The Kid*. Based on the places Charlie stayed as a child[21], it's an indicator of what life would have been like in their Pownall Terrace attic room

3 Pownall Terrace is the third door from the right

From the window, Hannah would imitate the street scene to Charlie and make up amusing stories about the characters and use brilliant facial effects, which Charlie became so adept at, to delight and ignite the talent of her son.

In 1951 Pownall Terrace was described:

> *Nos. 1 to 9 are built in yellow stock brick and are grouped on a line set at an angle to the roadway. They are of basement and three storeys, the basements extending forward to form a raised way. The lower windows and doors are set back slightly in semicircular recesses linked by stone impost bands. Above this level the fronts have been rebuilt in recent times, probably in replica of the original facades, which would appear to have dated from the early 19th century. The first floor cills are linked*

**The site of 3 Pownall Terrace today with the same London Plane tree
in both photographs**

*by a stone band and there is a simple cornice to the parapet.
These houses can be traced back in the rate books to 1790, but
it is improbable that much 18th century work remains. The
terrace perhaps takes its name from James Pownall who
occupied No. 3 in 1823.*[22]

It's a shame that such a significant address, which survived the war, no
longer exists. It's now a busy, noisy road next to a petrol station and this
would have been alien to Chaplin as he was born before the first car was
invented and, for that matter, the first moving pictures. Charlie's lifespan
was one of incredible times, not dying until after the first man walked on
the moon.

In the Lambeth archives there is a 1964 photograph of the building taken
shortly before its demolition as part of a Greater London Council

**Scene from *Easy Street* depicting the typical downtrodden entrance
lobby to a boarding house. This is likely what the entrance to
3 Pownall Terrace looked like**

redevelopment plan. It shows the ground floor windows and doors
boarded up and, in a prophetic irony to a famous scene in *The Kid*, the
first floor windows are broken from people throwing stones.

Whilst living here Hannah met an old friend who had become wealthy.
Charlie and Hannah got the chance to stay the summer at her house in
Lansdowne Square. The friend was the mistress of an old Colonel and the
young Charlie was quick to notice that a much younger man, also staying
in the house, always disappeared when the Colonel visited. When their
stay came to an end they returned to 3 Pownall Terrace. They left number
3 to briefly rent a room from a church member but there was a falling
out and so they returned once again to Pownall Terrace.

After his father's death in 1901, Charlie left school and, though yearning
to be an actor, tried to make money from odd jobs as a news vendor,

woodcutter, printer, toy-maker, glassblower and doctor's boy. These were tough times but his improvisation skills shone through just like the Tramp's wish to make a living. In *City Lights* the Tramp is in love with a blind flower girl and embarks on a series of hilariously told professions, whilst allowing her to believe him to be a millionaire, to pay for the restoration of her sight. One can see similarities with Chaplin's love for his ill mother and his attempts to help her by whatever means. In *Modern Times* the Tramp reveals the despair of the Great Depression in a succession of failed jobs and the audience are left with a clear picture of unemployment and poverty.

Charlie would have seen much of life from his experiences on the street. The pickpocket was a common thief of the Victorian streets and Chaplin used this in such films as *The Immigrant, The Idle Class, The Pilgrim, The Circus* and *The Kid* but always with that comic Chaplin twist. In *The Kid*, the destitute Tramp rescues a coin he did not know he had, that the

Scene from *A Dog's Life* likely influenced by the Chester Street area. On his 1921 return Charlie recalled an old tub outside stables where he used to wash

pickpocket had taken from him. Not satisfied with the return of the coin he guides his assailant's hands to his other pockets in the hope of uncovering more wealth. In *The Immigrant*, the Tramp is mistaken as a pickpocket when he attempts to secretly help an impoverished young woman by slipping money into her pocket. Not only is this the recollection of the pickpocket but again the concept of the Tramp and Chaplin as rescuers of women who have fallen on hard times.

While Sydney was at sea, earning good money on a passenger ship bound for Africa, he got an advance and the family moved to two rooms over a barber's shop in Chester Street, now Chester Way, literally just to the right of where you are now standing. However, the money soon ran out and they were back in, the seemingly ever available, attic room at 3 Pownall Terrace. There are two clues unfolding here. Firstly, 3 Pownall Terrace was probably in very poor condition, as the landlady does not appear to be able to let it to anybody other than Hannah. Secondly, Hannah was probably well known in the area and would get to hear of other places that were available. In Victorian times Lambeth would have had more of a village atmosphere, unlike the impersonal feeling one gets here now as the traffic streams through.

An escape of Charlie's, from these depressing rooms, was to the McCarthys who lived in a better part of Kennington Road. In Chaplin's autobiography he writes that the McCarthys had come to live in Walcot Mansions and he and their son Wally, the same age as Charlie, had formed an inseparable friendship:

> *As soon as I was through with school I would race home to Mother to find out if she needed any errands done, then race up to the McCarthys'. We would play theatre at the back of Walcot Mansions.*[23]

Charlie would often be invited to stay to tea, a source of nourishment for the boy. Walcot Mansions, now known as Walcot Gardens, can be found by walking further on up Kennington Road, passing Chester Way on your right then Walnut Tree Walk on the opposite side of the road, and standing with your back to number 167. Walcot Gardens are grand buildings and show the difference in wealth of the Chaplin family and that of the McCarthys. What also follows is that Pownall Terrace, housing the poor, would have been badly maintained which presumably led to its demolition, in the 1960s, and, ironically, has been replaced by ugly high rise buildings that also house the poor of Lambeth. Both West Square and Walcot Mansions, being more affluent, would have been better maintained throughout.

When Charlie got his first stage work with the Eight Lancashire Lads, he sometimes stayed at number 167, sleeping in the attic room with the son of the troupe's manager.[24] Now walk back to opposite the site of 3 Pownall Terrace.

During 1903[25] Hannah got word that Sydney, who was still at sea, had been put ashore at Cape Town with rheumatism. This likely would have ended Sydney's money coming through and she did not hear from him. Hannah became quiet and withdrawn. Half-starved, she let the single room become untidy and dirty. Letting her work go, the sewing machine was taken from her. Charlie returned home one day, from visiting the McCarthy's, to find an excited crowd telling him his mother had gone

Walcot Gardens

mad. Convinced that one of her neighbours was keeping Sydney from her, she'd been giving away lumps of coal as birthday presents for the children. Malnourishment, the fear of poverty, and the loss of her other son Wheeler probably caused her to confuse things. The parish doctor was called and Charlie led her back to Lambeth Infirmary, next to the workhouse. Charlie recalls:

> *When at last we arrived at the infirmary a young doctor took her in charge. After reading the note, he said kindly: 'All right, Mrs Chaplin, come this way.'*

She submitted obediently. But as the nurses started to lead her away she turned suddenly with a painful realisation that she was leaving me behind.

> *'See you tomorrow,' I said, feigning cheerfulness.*

> *They led her away looking anxiously back at me. When she had gone, the doctor turned. 'And what will become of you, young man?'*

> *Having had enough of workhouse schools, I replied politely: 'Oh, I'll be living with my aunt.'*[26]

Like in *The Kid*, where the authorities, against the judgement of the audience, take custody of an orphaned child, Charlie uses this theme again in *Modern Times*. The gamin, played by his third wife Paulette Goddard, becomes orphaned and her sisters are taken by the authorities but, like Charlie did here at the infirmary gates, made a rapid exit to avoid a similar fate. In his 1921 book, *My Wonderful Visit* Charlie confesses that he was terrified of dealing with officials when boarding a boat to England.

Charlie was alone, waiting for Sydney to return, living in fear of the landlady letting the room or her sending him to the parish authorities. One day Charlie got a telegram that Sydney would be arriving the next day at Waterloo Station. The unkempt Charlie had to break the news to Sydney that their mother was again at Cane Hill lunatic asylum in Coulsdon, Surrey, some twenty miles away.

The only delight was that Sydney had brought bananas and had twenty pounds, so the boys could survive awhile. Distance meant that it was hard

**Cane Hill was disused in the 1990s, and many of the vast buildings remained
in a derelict state until the start of redevelopment in 2008**

for the brothers to visit their very ill mother; when they did she was withdrawn, had lost her animated spark and was confined to a padded cell. She never really fully regained her mental faculties.

For the last seven years of her life Charlie moved Hannah to America where he surrounded her with sunshine and her favourite flowers. When she saw Charlie dressed as the Tramp, she wanted to buy him a new suit as she felt his costume rather tatty. She wanted to love and protect her boy until the end. In 1928, with her mind long gone she died, and Charlie recalled:

> *Even in death her expression looked troubled, as though anticipating further woes to come. How strange that her life should end here, in the environs of Hollywood, with all its absurd values – seven thousand miles from Lambeth, the soil of her heart-break. Then a flood of memories surged in upon me of her life-long struggle, her suffering, her courage and her tragic, wasted life ... and I wept.*[27]

What caused Hannah's illness is not fully clear. But she lost her husband to alcohol and to another woman, she failed in her legal bids to get support from him, her baby Wheeler Dryden was snatched by his father, she lost her singing voice, career and was plunged into poverty. Whether there was an actual illness or that just the combination of events was all too much for her to bear we'll never be fully sure.

Still in 1903, Charlie's yearn to be an actor drove him to register with Blackmore's theatrical agency off the Strand (he used the name for his fictional agent in his 1952 film *Limelight*). Arriving in worn-out clothes, he was surprised they even took his details. It was just one month after Sydney's return that he got a postcard asking him to call at the agency. He was given the part of Billy the pageboy in Sherlock Holmes for a tour of forty weeks, starting in the autumn, with the chance of a play, *Jim*, in the interim. Not only were the wages of two pounds ten shillings a windfall, but Charlie was struck by the kindness of the outfit he was joining. However, Charlie the ever shrewd businessman remarked, when being told the terms, 'I must consult my brother.' Sydney's response was, 'This is the turning point of our lives. If only mother was here to enjoy it with us.' Sydney promptly went to see Charlie's new employers asking for a rise! Later in America, Sydney would negotiate Charlie's first million-

Sydney Chaplin

dollar contract. Suddenly he was living his family's dream of acting and money.

In 1921, a friend Harry Charmain recalled:

> *We were pals as boys, and I held the book of words while he rehearsed and acted the part of Billy the page in Sherlock Holmes. Charlie was living at 3 Pownall-terrace, and we lived at No. 6. Charlie was badly off at that time, and he was always in and out of our house, and my mother gave him food and often shelter in cold and wet weather.*[28]

He goes on to say that Charlie would practise falling back down the steps of 3 Pownall Terrace and:

> *He was always funny, and he used to make all the boys and girls laugh. He used to perform plays in our house.*

Charlie's film performances sometimes show him smiling hopefully at, or walking in step with, somebody he wishes to gain favour from. These are simple childlike characteristics that form simple humour; that of a genius who learnt young how to appeal to old and young alike.

Jim was not a success; it received poor reviews and ran for just two weeks. However for Charlie it was a successful venture as he learned stagecraft, new techniques, and got many a good laugh and praise. This was his first real stage acting role as music hall was more a variety style of entertainment than a play.

Even though Charlie, the youngest member of the Sherlock Holmes Company, was lonely on tour, a poor grasp of spelling meant he was slow at replying to Sydney's letters. In exasperation Sydney wrote, 'Since Mother's illness all we have in the world is each other.' In his autobiography Charlie recalls being so moved by this he replied right away. The brothers remained very close until Sydney's death in 1965.

On returning from the forty-week tour, the boys took a better place on the Kennington Road. Charlie, now fourteen, was frequently in work and managed to obtain Sydney parts in the same plays. Hannah was in and out of Cane Hill yet well enough at one stage to join her sons on tour before retaking the flat over the barber's shop in Chester Street in the summer of 1904.[29] The boys would visit and stay when they could and Hannah discovered that Louise, her late husband's mistress, had died in Lambeth Workhouse. Out of kindness Hannah had been visiting Charlie's half-brother, the offspring of Charles Senior and Louise.

Sadly, in March 1905,[30] Hannah was admitted to Cane Hill asylum again. This time her problems could not be sorted and she remained there for seven years.

Note: To reach Cane Hill asylum alight at Coulsdon South station and take the footpath opposite. This goes uphill towards the new bypass, and then continues uphill on the other side of the road. Coulsdon South can be reached from London Victoria.

10. Kennington Cross

Walk the short distance further down Kennington Road to the junction with Kennington Lane. In Charlie's era this area was known as Kennington Cross. Charlie was not only a great actor, writer and director; he was also an accomplished musician, writing many of his own film scores. Charlie, in his 1921 visit recalled:

Kennington Cross where music first entered my soul.

Now noisy with traffic, it's hard to picture this location with Charlie's words:

It was here that I first discovered music, or where I first learned its rare beauty, a beauty that had gladdened and haunted me

Edwardian street scene of Kennington Road looking onto Kennington Park. This area now houses Barclays Bank and the Post Office

from that moment. It all happened one night when I was there, about midnight. I recall the whole thing so distinctly.

I was just a boy, and its beauty was like some sweet mystery. I did not understand. I only knew that I loved it and I became reverent as the sounds carried themselves through my brain via my heart.

I suddenly became aware of a harmonica and a clarinet playing a weird, harmonious message. I learned later that it was 'The Honeysuckle and the Bee'. It was played with such feeling that I became conscious for the first time of what melody really was. My first awakening to music.

I remembered how thrilled I was as the sweet sounds pealed into the night. I learned the words the next day. How I would love to hear it now, that same tune, that same way![31]

11. The Horns Tavern

Continue to make your way down the rest of Kennington Road, crossing Kennington Lane and following the signpost for Brighton, until you meet the junction with Kennington Park Road. A modern building now stands on the site of the Horns Tavern, on the opposite side to Barclays Bank and the Post Office.

About a year before the death of Charlie's father, William Jackson, the leader of The Eight Lancashire Lads, held a benefit for Chaplin Senior at The Horns. Jackson, who also lived on Kennington Road, was well known to the area and would have had no trouble in setting up this benefit show. Chaplin Senior, breathing with difficulty, made a speech whilst Charlie watched, standing on the side of the stage, not realising he was a dying man. Chaplin used this experience in *Limelight* where he plays Calvero, a clown who has lost his audience, who is given a benefit performance and

The Horns as Charlie would have known it

succumbs to a heart attack as he topples from the stage giving his final performance.

The Horns also acted as a meeting place, lecture hall and exhibition venue. In the eighteenth century this was the court of the Manor of Kennington and in the nineteenth century Surrey Cricket Club was founded here. In fact the Oval cricket ground is just a short walk away.

The site of The Horns Tavern today. The Horns was badly damaged during World War Two and the site was eventually cleared for redevelopment in the 1960s

12. Kennington Park

Now cross the road and enter Kennington Park.

When Charlie was living in this area his stage career was starting to take off, however we'll skip back to August 1898[32] to when Hannah played a crafty trick to see her boys at the Norwood school for the poor. Discharging herself from the workhouse she changed into her own clothes. She then returned to the workhouse where her sons were released into her care. They came here to Kennington Park and Charlie recalls:

> *Sydney had ninepence tied up in a handkerchief, so we bought half a pound of black cherries and spent the morning in Kennington Park, sitting on a bench eating them. Sydney crumpled a sheet of newspaper and wrapped some string around it and for a while the three of us played catch-ball. At noon we went to a coffee-shop and spent the rest of our money on a twopenny tea-cake, a penny bloater and two halfpenny cups of tea, which we shared between us. Afterwards we returned to the park where Sydney and I played again while Mother sat crocheting.*[33]

When they returned to the workhouse the authorities were not pleased, as they had to go through the admissions procedure all over again, including their clothes having to be steamed.

Just inside the park is a building commissioned by Prince Albert as a model house for the people of London. You can only wonder if Charlie, Sydney and Hannah dreamt of such a place when they visited on their day of escape from the workhouse. Walking into the park you'll note that the board display boasts a Charlie Chaplin adventure playground, on Bolton Crescent.

When Charlie turned eighteen his career encountered a lean patch. He tried a few things, including writing a comedy sketch and rehearsed with fellow actors at The Horns. It did not come to anything, and Charlie feared for his future as an actor/comedian. Then Sydney, who in 1906 had joined the renowned Fred Karno Company, managed to introduce Charlie to

Norwood, a workhouse school for Lambeth, located just south of Linton Grove on Elder Road, West Norwood. The lodge and front block are now the residential home 'Elderwood Place'. It is near West Norwood station which can be reached from London Victoria

Karno. Joining the Karno troupe was the dream of every budding comedian as it had roughly twenty productions. Charlie opened with *The Football Match* in early 1908.[34]

Charlie's career was now on a sound footing. His music hall popularity began to grow, from now there was no more turning back, no more poverty. From these nightly performances Chaplin would have learned what amused the audience. If one night he did not get a laugh at a particular moment, the next night he'd work on it and would get a laugh until it became intuitive. Working in the movies there is no live audience, nobody to roar with laughter. So by his intuitive knowledge of what humour worked, the retake was born. The audience was himself and he knew what to do at each stage to get the desired response. Prior to this, the economics of the movie industry, and the public's demand, required films to be made in just one take.

13. Kennington Gate

Now exit the park by the entrance where you came in, turn left and walk until you reach the major road junction. Cross towards the obelisk with the golden globe on top. This is Kennington Gate, a former tollgate on the Brighton Road.

With a steady income, the boys took a bachelor flat on the Brixton Road, which we'll visit later. It was a time when Charlie was working with one of the best touring companies in the country, performing at some of the best venues alongside some of the best stars of the day. But something was lacking for Charlie – love. Doing the rounds of the music halls he met a fifteen-year-old actress, Hetty Kelly. The nineteen-year-old Charlie plucked up his courage and asked for a date. They arranged to meet the following Sunday, at four o'clock at Kennington Gate. In his autobiography he describes a tense wait for her arrival followed by:

> *Then precisely at one minute past four, a young girl alighted from a tram-car, came forward and stopped before me. She was without make-up and looked more beautiful than ever, wearing a simple sailor hat, a blue reefer coat with brass buttons, with her hands dug deep in her overcoat pockets. 'Here I am,' she said.*[35]

He took her to the Trocadero where she would not eat a full meal and he was left ordering a meal with her watching. He bombarded her with love, asked her to marry him and devoted four pages of his autobiography to their eleven-day romance. Hetty's legacy stays on in his films of his love for younger women, and perhaps his personal life too.

Chaplin portrayed in the Tramp a man who falls in love at the drop of his derby hat but often is thwarted by a more manly or handsome suitor. One wonders if the loss of his mother's love influenced this and whether too this rebuff from Hetty allowed him to see himself, and the Tramp, as one not deserving of love. In his private life he frequently fell in love, perhaps seeking to replace that lost from his mother, leading him to a series of disastrous relationships: the first two of his four marriages left him close to breaking point. His attachment to Hetty was, perhaps, understandable.

Kennington Gate today

St Mark's and Kennington Gate circa 1830. The hut and gate across Kennington Park Road. An earlier incarnation of The Horns Tavern can be seen on the far right

Kennington Gate in the era of the tram-car where Charlie met Hetty Kelly

With his mother's affections long absent from his life, it would be a likely course to latch onto another.

Despite this setback in love Charlie continued to tour with Karno, even getting a spell in Paris.

14. St Mark's

Now cross the top of Camberwell New Road, by the crossing opposite the Oval Underground Station, to meet with the railings on the corner of St Mark's Church. Turn left and follow the railings around to the corner of Brixton Road and Prima Road.

In *City Lights* the Tramp falls in love with a blind flower girl who believes, through a simple misunderstanding, that the Tramp is a wealthy man. It was a scene that Chaplin, ever the perfectionist, made over three hundred takes of to get across what was in the artist's eye. Charlie would act out the scene for each of his actors. Every movement, blink of the eye was choreographed and demonstrated, and the shots were retaken

The railings of St Mark's Church. If you are not sure of the influence that the streets of London had on Charlie's film sets then you should visit here

and retaken until Charlie saw before him the vision that he had in his mind.

A flower girl would have been a regular sight of late Victorian London and, as Hannah loved flowers it was likely Charlie would have been familiar with them. Perhaps there was a blind flower girl on this corner?

For Chaplin, *City Lights* was his favourite film. By this time he was writer, star, producer, director and with the advent of sound he was now the composer of the synchronised soundtrack. He could afford all the takes in the world.

The film was a return to the London style, portraying a lonely city and two souls within it. The Tramp plays the rescuer of two people, the blind flower girl and that of a drunken millionaire he saves from a suicide bid. When the millionaire is drunk he takes the Tramp in, when he is sober the Tramp is rejected. One wonders if this relates to Charlie's father's alcohol problems (although Chaplin Senior rebuffed his son when drunk and was attentive when sober). It is possible that the millionaire's erratic behaviour, sometimes recognising the Tramp, at other times not, relates to how Hannah had been to Charlie when she was in the depths of her illness. More interesting, perhaps, is the relationship between Charlie and the blind flower girl. He scrimps and saves to pay her rent and to fund the restoration of her eyesight. The film was shot shortly after he lost his mother. Charlie's money could not restore Hannah to full health but in *City Lights* the Tramp manages to find the money to restore the girl's sight. It's possible that the deep-seated unresolved desire to rescue his mother was worked out through this film. Likewise the desire to pay the girl's rent, to save her from eviction, is again connected with his childhood and his desire to save his mother from penury.

Chaplin mentions in his autobiography how the marginalized and derelicts of society would be mocked by others on the streets. We see this with the boys and the pea shooter in *City Lights* where they taunt the Tramp for being a down-and-out. Also in the film we see the colliding worlds of poverty and wealth – the flower girl and the millionaire – with the Tramp flitting between the two. This is what he'd have seen in London with Hannah going from wealth to poverty, sometimes having glimmers of recovery, staying with wealthy friends, but then returning to destitution. This theme also comes up in *The Gold Rush* when the Tramp

**The scene from *City Lights* where the Tramp meets the blind flower
girl (Virginia Cherrill) — one of the most famous out of all the Chaplin films**

becomes a millionaire, then whilst modelling his old clothes for the press, is accused of being a stowaway and is faced with immediate poverty again. Yet, in frequent Chaplin style, he allows the audience to have what they want as the little guy is restored to his wealth. More powerfully in *City Lights* the girl, after her operation, becomes prosperous and we are left with the sense that somehow this creates a permanent distance between her and her now impoverished benefactor.

The concept of the millionaire, both in *City Lights* and *The Gold Rush*, are interesting themes for Chaplin. *The Gold Rush* was a poor man's dream of escaping poverty and would have been a common dream of the poor of late Victorian London. Yet Chaplin did become a millionaire, many times over, but he stayed true to that dream as a theme for his films. The subject also came up in an earlier film, *A Dog's Life*, made in 1918 in which Sydney featured. Charlie is a down-and-out who befriends a dog that digs up a wallet of money. Interestingly for this film too we can see that it draws on an incident from Charlie's childhood when he, Sydney and Hannah were living in poverty and Sydney found a purse full of money on a bus. In *A Dog's Life* we also see the classic T-shaped street scene of Lambeth and the little Tramp's dream of escape from the clutches of poverty. Furthermore the film portrays the recurrent Chaplin theme of two lonely 'oddballs' finding love and companionship in an otherwise lonely city.

15. Glenshaw Mansions

Glenshaw Mansions

Continue along Brixton Road until you pass South Island Place on your right. Amongst the shops you'll spy a number of entrances to Glenshaw Mansions. Stop at the communal entrance to numbers 9 to 16. If you ever wished to stand in Chaplin's footsteps then this is the place. Here, in 1908, Sydney and Charlie took number 15, a fine four-roomed flat. In his autobiography Charlie describes how they furnished it with pride and says:

> *We were able to engage a maid to come twice a week and clean up the flat, but it was hardly necessary, for we rarely disturbed a thing. We lived in it as though it were a holy temple. Sydney and I would sit in our bulky armchairs with smug satisfaction.*

We had bought a raised brass fender with red leather seating around it and I would go from the armchair to the fender, testing them for comfort.[36]

This is such an insight into the journey the boys had travelled, from poverty to their appreciation of hard-earned success. In modern day times we can relate this to a sudden win on the lottery. In Kennington Road Charlie had lived in a rundown terrace and would visit his friend, Wally who lived in the up market Walcot Mansions. Now Charlie lived in a building with 'Mansions' status. How proud he must have been.

By 1910 Charlie was getting outstanding press reviews and was selected to go on the Karno tour of America.[37] Also sailing to America was Stan Jefferson who later changed his name to Stan Laurel and found his own fame when he teamed up with Oliver Hardy. Stan and Charlie had already worked together in England, and they roomed together when on tour in the US. Incidentally Stan Laurel, Charlie Chaplin, Bob Hope and Cary Grant are all famous actors in American films yet they were all English. Cary Grant, like Chaplin, had an ill mother who he moved to the States.

In A.J. Marriot's *Chaplin Stage by Stage* he points out that in his autobiography Chaplin avoids mentioning the very famous people who worked with him such as Stan Laurel. He makes no reference to old sketches that he then used in his early movies and often quotes his successes as coming at a younger age than they truly did. Though Marriot is right to point these things out, and is a very astute biographer in doing so, it's worth pondering Chaplin's insecurity in doing this. As we have seen, Chaplin came from very desperate circumstances and his success was what kept him from the darkness of his past. When one's formative years have been difficult, one can have a deep fear of being returned to such difficulties. By referring to people that he worked with, who shaped his learning and the comedy sketches that he later used in his movie career (and one must remember that he was very inventive and many of his films were original) he, as an old man looking back at his life, perhaps feared that the public might view him differently. His fame and success were what divided him from the haunting draw of his childhood. To risk his success, even from an irrational fear, would have been too great.

Charlie became famous with his US audience for a portrayal of a drunk. This was in a sketch called *A Night in an English Music Hall* which was the American title of *Mumming Birds*, a popular sketch in the English music halls. Undoubtedly, the basis of the drunk was learned from his father, the music halls and streets of his childhood.

Charlie loved the vibrancy, positivity and freedoms that America offered. It was a reluctant young man who, in the summer of 1912 returned to England.[38] In his autobiography he recalled:

> *Sydney met me at the station and told me that he had given up the flat, that he had married and was living in furnished rooms along the Brixton Road. This was a severe blow to me – to think that the cheerful little haven that had given substance to my sense of living, a pride in a home, was no more ... I was homeless. I rented a back room in the Brixton Road. It was so dismal that I resolved to return to the United States as soon as possible.[39]*

Hannah was still unwell in Cane Hill. The boys visited but were unhappy with her treatment so, as they were able to afford it, they had her transferred to a private nursing home.

Charlie noticed the class divisions in England more and more. He toured London with the Karno American troupe but worried that he'd slip back into the clutches of poverty and obscurity. He was elated when the news of the next America tour came through. In his autobiography he recalled:

> *I loved England, but it was impossible for me to live there; because of my background I had a disquieting feeling of sinking back into depressing commonplaceness. So that when news came that we were booked for another tour in the States I was elated.[40]*

This is understandable when one has escaped a long-term unhappy experience. Any hint of being drawn back into such circumstances can bring on great panic. Chaplin later goes on to say:

> *Wealth and celebrity also taught me to spurn the insignia of the sword, the walking-stick and the riding whip as something synonymous with snobbery, to know the fallacy of the college accent in estimating the merit and intelligence of a man.*[41]

Charlie knew that only in America could he find the platform for his talents to reach their limit. In October 1912 Charlie set off for America again, this time sailing into New York. He could now be who he wanted to be and leave the London slums behind, though they would feature so much in his films. *The Immigrant* was a film that portrayed the arrival of lower class European immigration – not that Charlie suffered, as he was always affluent in America but he mixed his London experiences with the experience of America. In the film the only way he eats is by finding a coin on the street.

Chaplin continued to serve his apprenticeship on stage and was getting rave press reviews for his portrayal of the drunk. Mack Sennett, of Keystone fame, saw Charlie's performance and could see the laughs that Charlie got without speaking a word. This was perfect for the silent movie era and Sennett invited Charlie to join Keystone where he soon became the star with his improvisations and comic timing. Charlie was to use some of the Karno influence in his early films; none better than the depiction of a music hall in his 1915 film, *A Night in the Show*.

Charlie convinced Mack to give Sydney work and he therefore joined Keystone in 1914 and had success in his own right, though soon decided to devote his time to managing Charlie's business affairs.

16. The Ritz Hotel

Charlie was not to set foot on the streets of London again until as a visitor in 1921, 1931 and 1952. We'll complete our tour by visiting two of the significant places in those trips.

Retrace your steps back to Camberwell New Road. Turn left and walk to the Oval Underground station. Take the Northern Line, south for one stop to Stockwell where you should change onto the Victoria line North and alight at Green Park Station. This is on the edge of Green Park, opposite Buckingham Palace, the home of Queen Elizabeth II. Queen Elizabeth knighted Chaplin in 1975. Paul Merton, another south London comic, describes Chaplin as the knight that kicked the most arse. To literally kick an arse, especially a conveniently presented one, was the Tramp's weapon against arrogant social superiors. This was funniest in *The Kid* where the Tramp is seen training his young charge in how to effectively kick a conveniently placed behind.

Turn right out of Green Park Station, after following the Buckingham Palace exit signs, and walk a short distance up Piccadilly and you'll see The Ritz hotel in front of you. Pass along its front, cross the road at the corner with Arlington Street, and look up at the street sign of the same name. Compare the scene today with that of the picture of Chaplin waving to the crowds in 1921. Charlie elected to stay at The Ritz because it had been built when he was a boy and, now he could afford it, he was curious to know what it looked like inside.

This was Charlie's first visit back to London and came after completing *The Kid*. He'd wished to return to simply look around Kennington and Brixton but it soon became apparent, by telegrams and newspaper bulletins received on the sailing that this was by no means going to be a quiet visit. He had left in 1912 as a small star of the music hall and returned to great crowds awaiting him at Waterloo Station. What a contrast from when he'd met Sydney there, nearly twenty years beforehand, with the news that their mother was in Cane Hill. Charlie recalled:

> *Policemen on all sides. I am pushed and lifted and almost*

The Ritz today

dumped into the limousine. My hat is thrown in behind me. There are three policemen on each side of the car, standing on the running board. I can't get out. They are telling the chauffeur to drive on. He seems to be driving right over the people. Occasionally a head, a smiling face, a hand, a hat flashes by the door of the car.[42]

He goes on to say:

Now we are passing over Westminster Bridge. There are double-decked street cars. There's one marked 'Kennington'.

The newspaper headlines of the day included:

CHARLIE MOBBED IN LONDON

HOW THE FILM HERO CAME HOME

CHARLIE KISSED BY WOMAN ADMIRER

WINDOWS OF CAR SMASHED

AMAZING SCENES AT THE RITZ HOTEL[43]

It took forty policemen to get him into The Ritz where he acknowledged the crowd by making a little speech outside. Then he appeared at his window a number of times, the jubilant scenes perhaps reminded Londoners of Armistice Day.

> *It was for all the world like some Chaplin scen (sic) on the films but this time Charlie did not trip the policemen.*

Charlie at the Ritz 1921

**Charlie's arrival at The Ritz, 1921. On this visit crowds would form
wherever he visited. He was the world's first global superstar**

*All the roofs and windows commanding this scene were
overflowing.*[44]

He would receive seventy three thousand cards and letters, addressed to
him.

Overwhelmed, Charlie told friends he needed to rest then sneaked out
the back way to get to Kennington Road. In his autobiography he
recounts:

*The taxi turned a corner, and at last Kennington Road! There
it was! Incredible! Nothing had changed. There was Christ
Church at the corner of Westminster Bridge Road! There was
the Tankard at the corner with Brook Street (sic)!*

> *I stopped the taxi a little before 3 Pownall Terrace. A strange calm came over me as I walked towards the house. I stood a moment, taking in the scene. 3 Pownall Terrace! There it was, looking like a gaunt old skull. I looked up at the two top windows – the garret where Mother had sat, weak and under-nourished, losing her mind.*[45]

Charlie then revisited 287 Kennington Road, Kennington Park and Kennington Gate where he reflected on Hetty Kelly. Charlie recalled:

> *Hetty was the one audience from the past I should have liked to meet again, especially under these fantastic circumstances.*[46]

But alas it was on this trip he learned that Hetty had died. She had never really left his mind.

He then visited 15 Glenshaw Mansions and finally went for a drink at The Horns, the place of his father's benefit. Charlie recalls:

> *As I wandered through Kennington, all that had happened to me there seemed like a dream, and what had happened to me in the States was the reality. Yet I had a feeling of slight uneasiness that perhaps these gentle streets still had the power to trap me in the quicksands of their hopelessness.*[47]

What an amazing contrast to the poverty of his early years where he left anonymous and returned an international star. Yet the fear of losing what he had gained clearly haunted him.

In Charlie's 1921 book, *My Wonderful Visit* he describes his stay at The Ritz and nights out with friends, often not returning to the hotel until the early hours. On one occasion, he hitched a ride in a truck where the driver readily took to his celebrity passenger.

We mentioned above that this first return visit was just after Charlie completed *The Kid.* This film was a clear return to the streets of London and came at a difficult time for Chaplin. A newspaper of the day reported an elderly Mrs Harriet Tricks recalling knowing Charlie as a boy and remembering him sleeping in doorways. She went on to say:

When The Kid *film comes to Queen's Hall, Newington Butts, I am going to see it. From what I have been told about it there is no doubt he's playing his own life as a boy as near as possible. I can't read, but I have to form my own impression from the pictures I see, and I have often thought to myself, it's what he used to do and went through as a boy.*[48]

This visit had come just after Chaplin had lost his first-born and was going through a bitter divorce from his first wife, Mildred Harris. He and Sydney had just moved Hannah over to America and one wonders if nostalgia drew him back for a visit.

Charlie had come in for a degree of criticism for not having returned to fight in the Great War. The British government, realising his potential, spared him from slaughter on the battlefields, and instead used his popularity to sell Liberty Bonds. On this 1921 visit Chaplin wondered how his British audience would receive him. He need not have worried about his reception. As he walked the streets of Lambeth, crowds formed, surrounding him with warmth as he was amongst his own and crying out:

'Hello Charlie!' 'God bless you, Charlie!' 'Good luck to you lad!'[49]

We must remember this was soon after the devastation of the Great War where many of the young men were either killed or physically or mentally maimed. He went on to say:

If I can bring smiles to the tired eyes of Kennington and Whitechapel, if I have absorbed and understood the virtues and problems of those simpler people I have met … then this has been a wonderful trip.[50]

Chaplin took a risk in making a film about the war, the 1918 classic *Shoulder Arms*. Some doubted his judgement in parading himself as a hero of a war he did not fight in. Yet it was the Chaplin genius, in striking the balance between comedy and tragedy, that made this film such a success. He captures a group of German soldiers and mistreats the aristocratic German officer in charge. Once again he finds his level with the common man – German or English.

In his own life, Charlie must have been conscious of keeping that balance with the common man. On this visit he met the likes of H.G. Wells and the upper classes of society but he never lost that common touch.

On his 1931 visit he lunched with Sir Philip Sassoon at The House of Commons. He met Lady Astor in the lobby and was invited to lunch a few days later at 1 St James's Square, a short distance from here, with Bernard Shaw and others.

We can see by this stage that Chaplin was moving in high circles. On the 1931 trip he also met with the socialist prime minister, Ramsay MacDonald and had another meeting with Winston Churchill (they had met in the USA before on the set of *City Lights*). At this time Churchill was a backbencher, and throughout the thirties warned of the threat posed by Germany and Hitler. Perhaps it was this connection with Churchill that was the inspiration for *The Great Dictator*?

He also met with Gandhi near East India Dock Road. Gandhi discussed with Chaplin his anti-machinery feelings as he felt that they were a product of capitalism to control the masses. Charlie had previously been struck by a reference that profit comes out of wages. These insights possibly fuelled Chaplin's next film and last outing of the Tramp, *Modern Times*, which, like *The Great Dictator*, start to show how his later life experiences were influencing his films. Both of these films stayed true to experiences of his youth – falling in love and the portrayal of the downtrodden masses.

The main purpose of his 1931 visit was to promote *City Lights* and to see it premiered with Churchill and G.B. Shaw as guests. Torrential rain did not keep the fans away, though this time crowds were better policed than in 1921. He also returned to the Hanwell School and entertained the children with his antics. Chaplin was pleased to see that the children were now better off and he was moved by his reception.

17. Leicester Square

Return to Green Park underground station and take the Piccadilly line east to Leicester Square. Take Exit 2 out of the tube station and you'll notice The London Hippodrome above.

When Chaplin was working with the Eight Lancashire Lads, he was selected to play a cat in the Christmas pantomime, *Cinderella*, at The London Hippodrome where he played alongside the great French clown, Marceline. Charlie undoubtedly studied the body movements of this great man and, whilst playing the cat, became prone to improvisation – at one stage sniffing a stage dog's rear and cocking his leg to the roar of the audience.

In 1918 Charlie would again meet Marceline in Los Angeles but was shocked to see a faded star as just one of a number of clowns running around an enormous ring. Marceline later committed suicide. The fear of loss of one's audience stayed with Chaplin throughout his life, for in his youth, through the people he knew, it spelt destitution and a ticket to the workhouse. Charlie was aware of hearing older entertainers being referred to as 'through' and later committing suicide. These were people that sought the adulation of an audience to bolster a younger personality, so to lose it later in life left them with nothing. Millions in the bank would never detract Chaplin from this fear.

No better than in *Limelight* does Chaplin portray this inner fear of losing his audience. Charlie, playing the aged Great Calvero – a music hall 'Tramp Comedian' and clown, which one could easily understand was based on Marceline, has lost his touch, lost his audience. Set in 1914, in the world of the London music halls and Chaplin's own youth, it is as much about Chaplin's own ageing, and attendant fears, as the portrayal of a young dancer, played by Claire Bloom, who, having lost the use of her legs, is plunged into poverty and attempts suicide. One can draw the parallel with Hannah losing her voice and likewise being plunged into poverty. Calvero is a drunk and like Charlie's father has lost the ability to make people laugh, and thus his audience, as he succumbs to alcohol. Calvero takes the destitute dancer in and restores her to health, success and prosperity while his own fortunes fade.

We have a chance to see, for the last time, some of Chaplin's music hall performances set in the era he'd have known. A touching scene shows Calvero going from pub to pub, performing then collecting money. This scene is probably based on Chaplin's childhood where he witnessed performers down on their luck, going from pub to pub with the collecting hat only to be rebuffed by the successful and wealthy and reacting with a polite bow. This theme of deference comes up in how the Tramp was portrayed in love. In films such as *The Gold Rush*, the audience can see, through facial expression, his love for the girl, yet she is oblivious and drawn to another. The viewer is drawn to the plight and emotion of Charlie's characters, while his fellow players ignore his hurt and act according to their own wishes. For Charlie to actually lose that audience would have been the greatest fear of all. At some level it was what he held most dear.

Limelight was to be his last great film and, being set in the streets of his boyhood, is one of his most nostalgic for London. It features all we know to be classic Chaplin, nostalgia, lost love, hope, fears, romance, poverty and hunger. The pawnshop features again, with Calvero parting with his violin, his work tool, to pay for the dancer's medicine. There is also the infamous boarding house complete with an atypical landlady; stern yet with a sense of humour.

During the preparation for the film, the leading lady, Claire Bloom, recalled Chaplin openly admitting that his choice of wardrobe for her was styled on the favoured apparel of his mother and Hetty Kelly. He further drew on the memories of his mother by making the leading lady's own mother a dressmaker.

In *Limelight*, the theme of rescuing women (likely relating on his need to rescue his mother) has come up again. In *Modern Times* the Tramp stumbles across a young woman about to be detained for stealing a loaf of bread, and he steps in and claims to be the thief and is duly arrested. In *The Circus* he falls in love with and defends the daughter of a circus owner from her brutal father. Again in this film there's the fear of losing one's audience as the Tramp is only funny when not intended to be and not funny when intended to be. With his early leading lady, Edna Purviance, he took her from being a secretary to major film star, even writing *A Woman of Paris* for her to launch a career without him.

Now walk the short distance up Cranbourn Street into Leicester Square, the final visit of our tour and once the home of a number of music halls. The night before departing to America, in 1910, Charlie walked alone around the West End, pausing in Leicester Square, Coventry Street, The Mall and Piccadilly. He walked until two in the morning then returned home, was up at six and left a note to Sydney saying:

Off to America. Will keep you posted. Love, Charlie.[51]

Walk towards the prominent white statue of William Shakespeare above the fountain. To your right is the statue of our hero, Charlie Chaplin. A famous London square is a fitting place for a memorial to the great man and one is reminded of the popular music hall song 'If it's good enough for Nelson it's good enough for me.' The likeness is not the best, the reference to his age when he broke into films incorrect, and the left-handed Chaplin would have perhaps preferred the cane not to be in the right hand. But the derby hat, baggy trousers, cane and oversized boots are a genuine tribute to the man. It still captures the attention of the passer-by and is a popular place for tourists to pose for a photograph.

One might feel that with Shakespeare towering over him a lesser tribute was being paid to Charlie. Yet the diminutive Charlie was a man of the people and here you can stand alongside him as he'd have wished. Perhaps the British ruling classes that Chaplin would set out to mock prefer the elevated status of the Bard, yet both Chaplin and Shakespeare produced comedy for the masses. By the time Chaplin found his fame, Shakespeare had become the darling of the intelligent upper set and those that adored him regarded Chaplin as a lesser form of entertainer, appealing to the working classes. As time has passed, one can look back through wise spectacles and see Chaplin's work as timeless and true art, ironically no longer appealing to the masses of the modern working classes but instead to the lover of film art. Perhaps this is because the authorities that Chaplin so ridiculed, for their treatment of the downtrodden, have now long gone and have been replaced by a set who are sympathetic to the plight of the poor.

The parallel with Shakespeare ends here for Chaplin was true to his humble beginnings whereas Shakespeare shunned such topics and wrote of kings and nobility. Chaplin was never a fan of Shakespeare, preferring

The Chaplin statue in Leicester Square.
Note his slight frame, just five feet six and a half inches tall with narrow
thorax, all signs of malnutrition during his early development

instead Dickens who portrayed so well the impoverishment that Chaplin knew. Chaplin's own work, *My Autobiography*, was described by the BBC critics as 'comparable with Dickens', for this uneducated boy grew into the greatest filmmaker and one of the greatest wordsmiths of the twentieth century. Charlie was not only comparable with Dickens as a writer, both in autobiography and film script, but also comparable in the message to the authorities of the plight and suffering of the poor.

If Chaplin had never set sail for America he'd be an almost forgotten hero of the Edwardian music hall. It would have been unlikely he'd have succeeded in the British film industry, as connections opened more doors than talent. Instead it took the American film industry, financed by entrepreneurs not the ruling classes, to allow his innovation, and very English films, to shine. Only then did the powerful men of the world want to meet and be associated with Chaplin.

His three main returns to London were all after filming very nostalgic London-centric films (*The Kid* 1921, *City Lights* 1931 and *Limelight* 1952). *The Kid* and *City Lights* were after painful divorces and *Limelight* was after a painful and continual battle with the American authorities. Perhaps when Charlie was hit hard he was drawn to the bosom of his youth in his choice of film. One wonders if nostalgia drove him to make the films, or did making the films give him the nostalgia to return?

Behind the statue is the Empire Cinema where, during Chaplin's 1952 visit to London, he attended the opening of *Limelight*. Fittingly, for Chaplin, this was formerly a theatre and later the Empire Theatre of Varieties music hall; the 'Empire Theatre' sign can still be made out high up on the building and actually features as a venue within the film. Ironically in 1896 when Charlie first entered the workhouse[52], it played host to the first UK commercial theatrical performance of a projected film.

Limelight was Chaplin's last film to be made in America. An unfortunate series of misinterpretations led the authorities to rid themselves of a man they'd become convinced was a communist. In his film, *Modern Times*, Charlie had touched on a Marxist concern about the dehumanisation of labour, which started to firm the hate towards him. Sailing for Southampton with Oona, his fourth and last wife, and their then four children they received the news that his re-entry permit had been revoked. Chaplin had never sought American citizenship, which was a thorn to the authorities, yet conveniently became their way of ridding themselves of a man they'd loved then grew to hate for so called 'un-American' activities. In his autobiography he says:

> *Although I am not a communist I refused to fall in line by hating them.*[53]

Chaplin merely supported the rights of the downtrodden of society. In reality, like in *Limelight*, Chaplin had lost his American audience to the witch-hunts.

Once docked in Southampton, they caught the train to London. Charlie was amongst friends now and crowds were, like in 1921, waiting for him at Waterloo station. On this visit he stayed at the Savoy and visited 3 Pownall Terrace and 287 Kennington Road. He noticed then that 3 Pownall was boarded up, awaiting demolition.

Although the purpose of this visit was to show London to his wife and children it became a permanent exile, Chaplin returned to America only in 1972 to collect an honorary Oscar. In *Limelight* he portrays the fear and tragic consequences of losing one's audience. When the talkies came in, Charlie was afraid of losing his audience. After the Second World War cinema had moved on and Charlie's fan base was aging. In 1952 he had great success with *Limelight* yet he lost his American audience to the witch-hunts. The years between his films were growing and his final attempt, *A Countess from Hong Kong* (1967), was a flop, leaving Chaplin feeling very low. When in 1972, after the audience were shown extracts from his films, he received the longest standing ovation in Oscar history, it was no wonder, as a frail old man once more standing on stage, he appeared so very moved. He'd won his audience back. And with each new generation that comes along, Chaplin's work continues to find a new audience.

In an ironic twist, his musical score for *Limelight* won an Oscar in 1973. Having been banned, it was not released in Los Angeles until 1972 and was then eligible for Oscar nomination. The film where he played the clown who lost his audience did indeed win it back.

In this 1952 visit the family stayed at The Savoy. Charlie, in his autobiography says:

> *I pointed to the new Waterloo Bridge; although beautiful, it meant little to me now, only that it's the road to my boyhood.*[54]

He goes on to say:

> *Twenty years had elapsed since I had been here last. From my view the river bends and the contours of its banks have ugly, modern shapes that marred the skyline. Half of my boyhood had gone in the charred embers of its sooty, vacant lots. As Oona and I wandered through Leicester Square and Piccadilly, now adulterated by American gimcracks, lunch counters, hot-dog stands and milk bars, we saw hatless youths and blue-jeaned girls ambling about. I remember when one dressed the part for the West End, and strolled with yellow gloves and a walking-stick. But that world has gone, and another takes its place eyes, see differently, emotions react to other themes. Men weep at jazz, and violence has become sexual. Time marches on.*

Before settling in Switzerland, Oona returned to settle his affairs. Chaplin, the master of perception, had given Oona full signing authority just before they had sailed. Like the glass of water served by George Chapman, somehow Charlie had a sixth sense.

In later years Charlie would return and wander the streets of his youth. On one occasion he bumped into a young actor, who too was revisiting the streets of his youth. This young man was Michael Caine. Caine recalls:

> *One time, I remember, I ran into Charlie Chaplin who had been born there doing the same thing. I introduced myself and although I was by this time famous, he had obviously never heard of me, but we talked for a while and he seemed to have a tremendous nostalgia for the place and shared my sadness at the way the developers had torn it apart. About three hundred yards from the prefab where I grew up there was the ruin of an old Music Hall called the 'South London' and Chaplin pointed it out to me and told me that before he went to America he had appeared there in a show called* Mumming Birds. *It was a cold day and it may have been that, but I could swear that he had tears in his eyes. He obviously did not want to be disturbed*

for too long by a rather pushy young actor, so he said a rather
brusque goodbye and turned and walked away. He was a small
sad figure, and although he was wearing an overcoat and a
trilby hat, I could almost see the funny shoes and the walking
stick as he walked away, passing unnoticed through the crowds
of people who were the children of his past.[55]

In their autobiographies both Caine and Chaplin describe similar poor
dwellings of their childhoods, separation from their mothers (in Caine's
case wartime evacuation), how they both made it in the USA, both got
their brothers parts in their films and both had fathers who died in St
Thomas's hospital. The coincidence has a further twist in that they both
had half-brothers they did not know of until later in life. In Caine's case
the brother was handicapped and had spent his life in an asylum called
Cane Hill.

Charlie Chaplin died on Christmas Day 1977. The Times obituary referred
to Chaplin as having the 'common touch'.[56] Few words are better than
those from Wordsworth's *Immortality Ode* 'Or walk with Kings – nor lose
the common touch' for Chaplin did both. Fame never parted him from his
past and his films still show us that to this day. Charlie never lost sight
of his boyhood. Having come from poverty, he would never be able to
fully settle with the reality of his wealth.

Chaplin's fear was poverty and losing his audience, his weakness falling
in love, his dream wealth and his hope to rescue a pretty lady from the
clutches of some evil. London shaped this in him and the man and the
Tramp were often synonymous. It was a tragic irony that Oona, some
thirty-six years his junior, never was able to truly find a new life after his
death, she became withdrawn, and died of cancer in 1991.[57]

Charlie once said that anything anybody wanted to know about him could
be discovered from watching his films. His education for his films was
undoubtedly learned from the streets of London, the music halls and
stage shows. His movies chart his life better than any autobiography. I
hope this walk helps give an idea of how his childhood became those
movies.

With Hannah's training, his father's profession, what he witnessed on the
streets of Lambeth, his vaudeville training, it was a melting pot that has

given us the most wonderful films. Chaplin's life and films are like a five course meal with another unexpected course thrown in. With Chaplin there's never the thought that he could have done more or better. The little lad from Lambeth did good!

References

1 The Strand Magazine No. 325. January, 1918. Page 95

2 Charles Chaplin. My Autobiography. Page 13. Reprinted by
   permission of Association Chaplin

3 Charles Chaplin. My Autobiography. Page 13. Reprinted by
   permission of Association Chaplin

4 David Robinson. Chaplin His Life and Art. Page 10

5 David Robinson. Chaplin His Life and Art. Page 15

6 David Robinson. Chaplin His Life and Art. Page 13

7 David Robinson. Chaplin His Life and Art. Page 16

8 Charles Chaplin. My Autobiography. Page 19. Reprinted by
   permission of Association Chaplin

9 Charles Chaplin. My Autobiography. Page 19. Reprinted by
   permission of Association Chaplin

10 Charles Chaplin. My Autobiography. Page 58. Reprinted by
   permission of Association Chaplin

11 Charles Chaplin. My Autobiography. Page 9. Reprinted by
   permission of Association Chaplin

12 Charles Chaplin. My Autobiography. Page 22. Reprinted by
   permission of Association Chaplin

13 Charles Chaplin. My Autobiography. Page 26. Reprinted by
   permission of Association Chaplin

14 Charles Chaplin. My Autobiography. Page 56. Reprinted by
   permission of Association Chaplin

15 David Robinson. Chaplin His Life and Art. Page 722

16 Charles Chaplin. My Autobiography. Page 33. Reprinted by
    permission of Association Chaplin

17 Peter Haining. Charlie Chaplin A Centenary Celebration. Page 24

18 Charles Chaplin. My Autobiography. Page 40. Reprinted by
    permission of Association Chaplin

19 Charles Chaplin. My Autobiography. Page 50. Reprinted by
    permission of Association Chaplin

20 David Robinson. Chaplin His Life and Art. Page 721

21 Charles Chaplin. My Life in Pictures. Page 188

22 The Survey of London: volume 23: Lambeth: South Bank and
    Vauxhall (1951), pp. 128-136 (Author: Sir Howard Roberts and
    Walter H. Godfrey (editors)) Copyright © 2007 University of
    London & History of Parliament Trust — All rights reserved

23 Charles Chaplin. My Autobiography. Page 67. Reprinted by
    permission of Association Chaplin

24 "A.J" Marriot. CHAPLIN Stage by Stage. Page 16

25 David Robinson. Chaplin His Life and Art. Page 42

26 Charles Chaplin. My Autobiography. Page 70. Reprinted by
    permission of Association Chaplin

27 Charles Chaplin. My Autobiography. Page 284. Reprinted by
    permission of Association Chaplin

28 The Star (No. 10412) 2nd September 1921

29 "A.J" Marriot. CHAPLIN Stage by Stage. Page 55

30 David Robinson. Chaplin His Life and Art. Page 724

31 Charlie Chaplin. My Wonderful Visit. Hurst & Blackett Ltd. 1921
    Page 92. Reprinted by permission of Association Chaplin

32 David Robinson. Chaplin His Life and Art. Page 722

33 Charles Chaplin. My Autobiography. Page 28. Reprinted by
    permission of Association Chaplin

34 "A.J" Marriot. CHAPLIN Stage by Stage. Page 88

35 Charles Chaplin. My Autobiography. Page 104. Reprinted by
    permission of Association Chaplin

36 Charles Chaplin. My Autobiography. Page 102. Reprinted by
    permission of Association Chaplin

37 "A.J" Marriot. CHAPLIN Stage by Stage. Page 121 and 134

38 "A.J" Marriot. CHAPLIN Stage by Stage. Page 240

39 Charles Chaplin. My Autobiography. Page 132. Reprinted by
    permission of Association Chaplin

40 Charles Chaplin. My Autobiography. Page 133. Reprinted by
    permission of Association Chaplin

41 Charles Chaplin. My Autobiography. Page 267. Reprinted by
    permission of Association Chaplin

42 Charlie Chaplin. My Wonderful Visit. Hurst & Blackett Ltd. 1921.
    Page 74. Reprinted by permission of Association Chaplin

43 The Star (No. 10419) 10th September 1921

44 The Star (No. 10419) 10th September 1921

45 Charles Chaplin. My Autobiography. Page 265. Reprinted by
    permission of Association Chaplin

46 Charles Chaplin. My Autobiography. Page 263. Reprinted by
    permission of Association Chaplin

47 Charles Chaplin. My Autobiography. Page 266. Reprinted by
    permission of Association Chaplin

48 The Star (No. 10412) 2nd September 1921

49 Charlie Chaplin. My Wonderful Visit. Hurst & Blackett Ltd. 1921
    Page 88. Reprinted by permission of Association Chaplin

50 Charlie Chaplin. My Wonderful Visit. Hurst & Blackett Ltd. 1921
    Page 220. Reprinted by permission of Association Chaplin

51 Charles Chaplin. My Autobiography. Page 118. Reprinted by
    permission of Association Chaplin

52 David Robinson. Chaplin His Life and Art. Page 721

53 Charles Chaplin. My Autobiography. Page 458. Reprinted by
    permission of Association Chaplin

54 Charles Chaplin. My Autobiography. Page 456. Reprinted by
    permission of Association Chaplin

55 What's It All About? By Michael Caine, published by Century.
    Reprinted by permission of The Random House Group Ltd.
    Page 34

56 The Times "Great Lives. A Century In Obituaries". Page 388

57 David Robinson. Chaplin His Life and Art. Page 694

List of Illustrations

Unless listed below all photographs are copyright the author or are from the author's own collection. If anyone has claim to the copyright of any of the photographs, or illustrations, not listed below please make a representation to the publishers such that appropriate acknowledgement can be made in any subsequent edition.

P49   Street scene still from *Easy Street*

P51   Pavement scene still from *A Dog's Life*
        © Roy Export SAS

P53   Attic room scene from *The Kid*
        © Roy Export SAS

P54   Pownall Terrace
        By kind permission of "A.J" Marriot

P56   Entrance porch still from *Easy Street*

P57   Street scene still from *A Dog's Life*
        © Roy Export SAS

P61   Cane Hill
        By kind permission of Ben Charlton

P63   Sydney Chaplin
        © From Roy Export Company Establishment archives

P69   The Horns
        Reproduced by kind permission of Lambeth Archives
        department

P79   Railing scene stills from *City Lights*
        © Roy Export SAS

P87   Balcony scene still from Chaplin at The Ritz in 1921
        From the Blackhawk Collection of the Topical Budget newsreel
        footage entitled "Charlie" on the Ocean. Grateful thanks to
        David Shepard, owner of the Blackhawk Collection.

P88   Street scene still from Chaplin at The Ritz in 1921
        © Roy Export Company Establishment archives

Bibliography

Books in print:

My Autobiography
Charles Chaplin
Summary: Chaplin's autobiography, first published in 1964.
ISBN 978-0-141-01147-9
Penquin Books Ltd

Chaplin Stage by Stage
Summary: This volume contains detailed research of Chaplin's stage
work prior to entering films.
"A.J" Marriot
ISBN 0-9521308-1-5
Marriot Publishing
20, Oughton Close
Hitchin, Herts. SG5 2QY

Books out of print:

Chaplin His Life and Art
Summary: A detailed biography
David Robinson
Penquin Books Ltd

My Wonderful Visit
Summary: Chaplin's description of his 1921 visit to London.
Charlie Chaplin
Hurst & Blackett Ltd

Charlie Chaplin A Centenary Celebration
Summary: A biographical work based on contemporary articles.
Peter Haining
W Foulsham & Co Ltd

My Life in Pictures
Summary: A book of pictures of Chaplin's life with captions by the great man himself.
Charles Chaplin
Bodley Head

DVD:

Charlie Chaplin Complete Box Set
Warner Home Video
DVD Release Date: 22 Sep 2003
ASIN: B0000AISJG

Chaplin Revue
Warner Home Video
DVD Release Date: 15 Aug 2005
ASIN: B0009EMOII

Unknown Chaplin
Network
DVD Release Date: 8 May 2006
ASIN: B000F5S200

Acknowledgements

Grateful acknowledgments are due to: Kate Guyonvarch (Association Chaplin), Claire Byrski (Association Chaplin), Anne Ward (Lambeth Archives Department), Jane Pendry (proof reader), Nancy Stanger (proof reader), Gisella Storm (proof reader and walk tester), "A.J" Marriot (author Chaplin Stage by Stage), Ben Charlton (Cane Hill historian), Kate Burry (Cane Hill photographic research), The staff of the British Library Newspaper Reading Room at Colindale, David Shepard (Blackhawk Collection) and Gabrielle White (The Random House Group Ltd).